Silk City Sparrow

by
Eileen Moeller

Published by

Copyright 2020 Eileen Moeller.

All rights reserved.

Published by Read Furiously. First Edition.

ISBN: 978-1-7337360-7-7

Poetry
Poetry Collection – Single Author
Memoir
Women Writers
New Jersey

In accordance with the U.S. Copyright Act of 1979, the scanning, uploading, and electronic sharing of any part of this book without the permission of the publisher or creator is forbidden.

For more information on *Silk City Sparrow* or Read Furiously, please visit readfuriously.com. For inquiries, please contact samantha@readfuriously.com.

Cover design by: Adam Wilson

Edited by Samantha Atzeni

Read (v): The act of interpreting and understanding the written word.

Furiously (adv): To engage in an activity with passion and excitement.

**Read Often. Read Well.
Read Furiously**

To my three stalwart brothers: Tom, Chuck, and Mike Daly who know many of these stories, but not all, and who have many of their own. And to our parents, Tom and Marilyn, who gave us everything they could.

Acknowledgements

Many thanks to the editors of Read Furiously, Adam Wilson and Samantha Atzeni, for their generosity in getting this work out there, and for their love of narrative and New Jersey. And undying gratitude to Jersey poets, Thank you to BJ Ward for reading the book, and for his kind words. Maria Gillan, and Joe Weil for their encouragement of my work, and for inspiring and mentoring me from afar.

Earlier versions of the some of the poems appeared in the following:

"Confessions", – Footwork 1987; "Tree of Heaven" and "When The Junk Man Came Down Summer Street" – Outerbridge"1987; "We Learn About Love" – Passaic County Community College Anthology 1992; "The Hunger Angels", Winner of the Dorothy Damon Award – Poetpourri 1992; "The Circus Comes To Paterson" as "Circus" in Feminist Studies, vol. 28, No. 2, Summer 2002; "The Girls On Cedar and Summer" in Paterson: A Poet's City, 2005; "Aunt Aggie Closes Her Eyes" and The Circus Comes To Paterson" in The Paterson Literary Review, issue 34, 2005;, "The Sleeping Beauty" in Women. Period, a Spinster's Ink anthology. 2008, and in Gretel Turns Sixty, a contemporary music CD, by composer Dale Trumbore, 2011; "My Mother And My Father" – 50 Over Fifty: A Celebration of Established and Emerging Women Writers ed. Carla Spataro, PS Books, 2016. "O Paterson" and "Silk Mill Sopranos" – The World Takes: Life in the Garden State, Read Furiously, 2019.

Of All the Birds

It's the sparrows she likes best.

Brown jacketed survivors,
living on the fringes,
hopping from tree to bush to sidewalk,
finding seeds and berries,
but also cake crumbs,
puddles of ice cream,
the errant bread crust.

Sparrows watching humans,
taking what comes,
adapting to city life.
Seizing the moment:
anything worth a peck or two.

She wonders if we're gods to them,
doling out a daily measure of stingy blessings,
whether they pray to us, like we do, to ours,
always begging and pleading
for control of what comes our way.

No. Their chirps seem more like hosannas.
The way they sing to the day's light
as it comes and goes After all,
what more do they need, as they
suddenly lift into flight?

Table of Contents

Silk City: Sandy Hill
O Paterson
Summer
The Girls On Cedar and Beech
The Duchess
Santa Croce Camarina
Early Memory
Genevieve
First Communion Girl
We Were Little Coyotes
Magnolia
School 15
At Saint Anthony's
What I Learned in School
When The Junk Man Came Down Summer Street
Milk
Crows
Mary Coates
Confirmation
Dominic Savio
Boys And Girls: The Rules
Like a Scrub Pine
Hunger Report #10
Fig
The Circus Comes To Paterson
Columbia
Santa And Rosa
Confessions
Nun Lore

Warp and Weft
Five Years Old
Tex
Turtle Girl
Water Office

The Hunger Angels
We Learn About Love
Dee Dee And Pop Pop
Sleeping Beauty
Hardware
Phoebe
Uncle Charlie
Uncle Joe
Silk Mill Sopranos
Nana's Blue Jay Sisters
Mouse Pie
Rough Cut
The House They Bought On Summer Street
Sleeping Beauty
Blessing of the Throats
Auntie Ee
Aunt Mary
Red
Sonia and Tamara
Georgette
Sister Mary
Women As Big As the World
Smoke
Goodbye House
On the Bus: N. Straight St.
On the Bus: To the Indian Black Mustache
On the Bus: Rebirth
My Mother and My Father
There I Am In 1966
Sister Marietta
Poem for Dottie
Senior Year
On Catskill Mountain Vacations
Paterson by Milk Light
Aunt Aggie Closes Her Eyes

Silk City: Sandy Hill

O Paterson

Your windows steal light,
as the past pants and wanders
block after gritty block,
begging for love.

City of bright filaments,
where Allen Ginsberg came
into flower, where Doctor Williams
spent the idle hour between house calls.
Where men smooch the air, where
silk mill sopranos lament over blue teacups,
invisible as the door in a rabbit.

I can't go there.
I can't go back there any more.

City of silk left unfinished,
where mills sit like mothers,
pining for their many lost children.
Your glory flown far away.

The mighty Passaic trembles
in its fur before it falls.

Summer

The houses were lined up shoulder to shoulder,
as if they were holding each other up against the fray.
Their high porches added some dignity, but mostly they looked
tired, hemmed in by chain-link fences with broken gates,
and punctuated by the dark mystery of alleyways tunneling between.

Here and there, a three or four story tenement towered over the rest,
long narrow apartments on each side of a hallway, making them
look like double-breasted suits with blue flagstone shoes.
Small stores gave color to every block, cheap creamy cups,
and metal colanders at the Scalvino's, red long-johns at Goodkoop's,
barber pole stripes at Carlo's, posters and ocean liners at the Travel agent's.

These were the faces we presented to the world: modest and utilitarian,
and most of all, weary of the hard labor it took to buy them,
to own anything, especially these houses small as they were.
Dirty work, done in smelly dye houses, airplane foundries,
sweat shops, and mills so loud you couldn't speak without shouting.

But the back yards, oh the back yards were another story.
Hidden behind what might look like surrender,
were little Edens, full of climbing roses, huge boxwood
hedges, their leaves thick and pungent, mammoth pear trees,
peach trees covered in juicy yellow fists, twisting ivy vines,
and lush gardens full of zucchini blossoms, squash,
cucumbers, peppers, and tomatoes. Everything
heavy with the promise of nourishment,
the intimacy of back porches, our neighbors no longer
wearing their pinched street faces, as they hung clothes
out, or leaned over the fence to chat, relaxed and fully themselves.

So what if all anyone, passing by, could see were rows of squatty
houses, and the stooped backs of the working poor, crawling into them
every night, to feed and rest. It was none of their goddamn business.
And we all did our best to keep our measure of beauty to ourselves.

The Girls On Cedar and Beech

had names like songs,
like arias in fact,
that rose and fell
in handfuls of confetti across the sun.

Santa and Rosa,
tucked like a holy picture
inside your missal,
Teresa, Angela, Gracia,
church bell glitter falling
like the angels as they sing us into evening,
Sylvia, Stella, Maria
gleaming in moonlight.

Immacolata Concezione!
Palmyra! Preciosa!
Like hymns the mother's voices
rang down the sidewalk
and girls we called Connie and Pam and Sina
dropped the end of the jump rope
and became a soft percussion of steps,
a murmur of acquiescence,
the creak of a screen door.

Christiana who got to watch the nuns eat in the convent
because her mother cooked for them,
Carmella carrying altar lace,
Caterina celestial in her wedding cake Sunday dresses,
Cosmina and Mariana graceful as boats adrift at sea.

All of them except me.

Ei ─────leen !
My mother bellowed,
with an emphasis on the "eye",

her voice at full tilt,
rain-lashed and battered
as the Irish cliffs in a storm,
smoky as their pubs every night of the week.
The street went silent all of a sudden,
As the girls I turned my back on, made the sign of the cross,
and I took the longest way home I could.

The Dutchess

That's what Patsy across the street
called my grandmother. She lived
in the tenement on Cedar Street, a floor
below the Donahues, the other outsiders.

She'd been an English governess for the wealthy
on Long Island, when my grandfather took
the ferry from New Haven to see the cook
he's been wooing, until he met her, and fell
flat-on-his-face in love. She was only nineteen
when he briskly made her his Mrs. and brought
her here, to Sandy Hill, along with his mother,
for companionship, to that cold water flat
of what they called railroad rooms,
my father already quickening.

They lived there thirty-seven years,
raising five pencil-thin children, who
towered over the rest of the neighborhood.
When the old man died, she found $800.00
in his sock drawer, though he'd often
denied her food money.

Patsy watched her head to six-thirty mass
every morning, tall, thin, and proper,
despite her ratty old coats and thick-heeled shoes.
He pictured her pouring tea into blue china cups,
gracious and regal, though she seemed to
move within a cloud of sadness.

Once the youngest boy grew big enough,
he accompanied her, arm in arm,
around the corner, as the church
bells rang. Patsy could set his clocks
by their passing: the Duchess of Sandy
Hill, and her Bonny Prince Charlie.

Santa Croce Camarina

hovered like a dream
we couldn't share,
though the neighbors tried
to describe its tile floors
and olive trees,
its churches
overlooking each square,
gave us tastes of it
in fried zucchini flowers,
cacciatore, pizza frite,
acacia, dusky homemade wine.

Their backyard gardens
bristled with vitality, whispered
this is what it was like, only beautiful,
their pigeon coops on stilts trilled and cooed,
their hunting dogs barked its praises,
their fig trees murmured seductions.

They had a club in a yellow brick
building on 20th Avenue,
as mysterious to the rest of us,
as the tiny marching
band of older men
with dented horns,
that made the rounds
on San Giuseppe's Day.

Mysterious as 21st Avenue, with its live
rabbits and chickens hunched
and fluttering in wooden crates,
its fish swimming in aerated tanks
waiting to be brought home
and killed for dinner, just like they
did in the old country.

Early Memory

Standing harnessed in the carriage
as my heavily pregnant mother
pushes it down the street.

Going to buy another pack of the cigarettes
she will smoke by the window
lost in the thousand daydreams
it takes to keep her from bolting.

We'll be waiting for Daddy,
who always stops at his mother's first,
and then for a couple of short ones
at one of the neighborhood taverns.

I sit playing at her feet. Every once in a while,
she gives me a soft uh-huh, in response to
my constant chatter to dollies, the endless
namings, my tugs at the hem of her housedress.

At sixteen months old, I am already talking in sentences,
surprising a well-dressed man who's stopped to bow
to the Bella Madonna, to offer a shiny penny
a la bambina so she can buy something
dolce at the local soda fountain.

I stare at the little brown thing in
his hand, look him in the eye and say,
I'd just as soon have a nickel,
which finally wakes Mommy up,
so she smiles and shakes her head,
and this shows off the beautiful dimple
I love, but see too little of.

Soon my brother will be born, and I
will become a watcher, but I will keep
this moment tucked away: this man and
my mother laughing so hard at what I said,
me jumping like a happy monkey between them.

Genevieve

was left at our house
by the Easter bunny,
mother said. Just like
the tiny chicks and ducks
who lived a day or two,
and then died, only Genevieve
stayed alive and became our pet,
hopping around the kitchen,
and begging at the table.

She lived in a box behind the stove,
was paper-trained, and sat in my
mother's lap to let us pet her.
Until our landlord came to collect
May's rent, and told us pets
weren't allowed. He gave
my mother a couple of days
to get rid of her, and when she did,
she told us Genevieve went
to live on a farm, where she could
eat right out of the garden, and
snuggle with other animals.

The following weekend, Tommy and I
were sent out to play, and when we
climbed up the slope of our cellar door,
we could see two bigger kids running
up and down Mrs. Varcadipane's steps.

Turns out they were her grandchildren.
They told us this when we waved and asked
what they were up to. They'd come for dinner
and soon there would be dessert. When we said
who we were, the girl got a funny look on her face.

She nudged the boy and he said, we ate your rabbit,
plain as day. The two of us stood there in disbelief,
until I pretended I heard my mother calling us in.
We turned and headed back to the porch,
and sat holding hands beneath the windows
trying to contain this new and enormous silence.

First Communion Girl

Her hands, encased in their ruffled organza gloves,
hold each other tenderly, as if for the first time.

A bow grabs at the corner of each of her eyes, and the veil's corona
rays out around her face as if it were the only source of light.

She stands near a shabby fence,
fat white rabbit, golden edged

prayer book, bridelet, cupcake,
the shadows forming a miniature road beside her.

This is the way the angels go, she thinks,
still feeling the tickle of wings, the papery taste of the host.

From now on she will be Milky Way, milkweed, white birch,
wrensong weaving its way through the hedgerow.

Lift me, gather me in, she wants to say,
but doesn't know why.

Behind her, in the playground, a lone swing
dangles, twisted and broken.

Some people walk by
with a dog as big as a wolf.

We Were Little Coyotes

Playing tricks whenever she
seemed to be slipping too far away.

If we woke up, and she'd gone to the store
we rubbed our bodies with her lipstick,
or took their satin quilt out into the yard,
so we could roll around in the snow
in our footed pajamas without getting wet.

If we came home after school to an empty house,
we threw bananas into the fan, to try to slice them,
the way Popeye did baloney, dealing the slices
like cards between slices of white bread.
After that, globs of banana hung from
the kitchen ceiling, and encrusted the walls
for a week, before either one of them noticed.

If she left us with the woman next door,
we remembered we needed a paper
we'd left inside the locked house,
climbing in the living room window,
to fetch it, and knocking over a lamp
or the Christmas tree, so bits of broken
glass glittered the rug, and ornaments hung
broken, like a year's worth of calamities.

The worst kids in the world. Two hapless
beasts in big trouble, and skulking around her.
Bent on filling an absence that drove us wild.

Magnolia

The one and only time
we went to the park with Daddy,
I swung so high and long it made me sick,
so I had to lie down on a bench,
and when I stared at them sideways,
the swings heaved in
and out like shallow breaths,

so Tommy became a blur,
a dream on the merry go round,
until he suddenly fell, given over
to the pull of dark forces at work that day,
and landed splat in a mud puddle.

He was soaked and mucky from head to toe.
so Daddy said, we'd have to leave right away,
made us wade ankle deep through bruised pink
blossoms all the way to the parking lot, where
Tommy didn't like it, when Daddy stripped him
down to his underwear so he wouldn't ruin the upholstery.

As we headed home, Tommy cried himself to sleep
as I held him close, the two of us lost in the Pontiac's
velvet gloom, and the roar of Daddy's silence.

School

Sat at the top of Sandy Hill itself,
looming over the houses
like a red brick prison.

Our parents wouldn't let us
go there, enrolling us in
Catholic school instead.

They said it was too rough,
the kids carried knives.
We'd get picked on
for being too smart.
It was out of our league.

Most of the kids we knew
went there. They threw boulders
at each other, and said lots of
words we weren't allowed to say.

When we climbed the hill to play
by the Monkey Tree, we sent a scout
to make sure no one else was up there.

Sometimes, in my dreams, all the bad kids
were locked up, and could never come out.
Sometimes, it was me, trapped inside
a tiny box, without anyone to play with.

At Saint Anthony's

During assembly, it was always the filigree girls,
drifting like little boats up to the stage to sing,
silver and cool as fountains in empty piazzas.

Miraculous Medal May Crowning girls
like Rosa Trama, whose hair billowed out in
Mediterranean waves, sweeping us back to
Sicily, to the harbor in Santa Croce Camarina,
on the wings of the *Ave Maria*, its echo leaping
like dolphins along the church basement floor,
the silence that followed, fuzzy as grape leaves
whispering against the wooden slats of the arbor

or Maria Buscema, thin and reedy, her voice, husky
straw grass on red dust hills, her hair haloing a porcelain
sundappled face. Maria in her white Communion dress
on an open balcony, standing beside a faded blue table
fingering her rosary, curtains blowing around her
like angels, her song a swallow, lending us grace.

Ari Viderci Roma poured through the air,
and down the cheeks of the nuns,
while the rest of us pretended to play
the accordian, its heavy chest wheezing in time,
its mother of pearl fingerboard spelling out
our own little cantos of yearning.

What I Learned in School

Do not try to stop one girl from hitting another. It might be her sister.

Crying Walter hates to talk in front of the class.

A boy might suddenly kiss you, when he's passing out the homework.

Do not tell Louie to call Grandma on the pencil sharpener.

Going to school late, you can sit outside until it's lunchtime.
Then go home for lunch, and come back, saying
your mother forgot to give you a note.

Do not come home early because a stray dog
might bite you and get you into big trouble.

You always know what to do and when to do it.
When you are done with your work, sit with
your arms folded, and your lips locked.

The sisters always pay attention, even when you think they are busy.

If you don't have to go when everyone lines up,
you might wet your pants on the cold walk home.

Reading and writing are fun. If you are a good reader,
you might get to read aloud to the class when Sister is tired.

If you have to sit on a boy's lap in the car,
put a telephone book under you first.

Do not skip Sunday mass. Sister will tell the class
your envelope was not in the basket.
Do not lose your uniform belt, or you'll look like a slob.

Wear a coat when it's cold, or you'll look like nobody's child.

No matter how good your report card is, your brother's will be better.

When The Junk Man Came Down Summer Street

We stood on the sidewalk, across from
the corner drugstore, eyeing our own reflections
in the green glass doors behind which Doc's
Great Dane slept every night to scare away burglars.

We stretched and pranced impatient as runners,
waiting for the junk man and his wagon to roll
like a ghostly wave across Doc's little harbor of
marble and glass, the knobs on the soda
fountain, bobbing like white marker buoys.

We followed him down the block then:
past old D'Alessandro squinting
through Coke bottle glasses
his white hair stiff as the brushes
that hung from the sides of the wagon,
past Rose Quatrocchi with her
sons in their shiny red stroller,
past Ralph Molinaro who kept
pigeons and rabbits, his backyard
bursting with edible blossoms,
past the girls playing hopscotch
with a hard rubber heel, begged from
the shoemaker who never seemed busy,
who my father said was a Mafia bookie,
their game interrupted, the girls ran behind us.

The junk on the wagon tilted and swayed
like the graceful trombones and bugles
the old men played as they marched
on the feast of *San Rocco*. His cowbells
were strung like stars across our daylight.
They clanked and tinkled and floated a
rhythm that made us start skipping.

There was Santa and Rosa whose mother
could never remember their names, and called
them *Hey You* in Italian, Columbia who couldn't
come out unless Baby Jerry came with her,
Tanya and Sonia, and Hanna their sister,
their mother at the window in her flowered babushka.

Then Georgie Capello and blonde-headed Victor,
and Sammy the Mongol, who swore like a trooper.
Even crazy Pepino in his black leather jacket,
stopped combing his hair, and came out
to call to the chestnut junk wagon horse,
who seldom looked up at the sound of our voices,
his hooves rocking slow on the tarry macadam,
his rickety legs inching everyone down to the corner.

Past the brick stoop where Gracie's
communist tenant sat smoking a stogie,
past Father Andresani's cranky old mama
her gray head nodding in time to the rosary,
down to Louie's where we bought cigarettes,
for Daddy, and lemon ice with the leftover money.
Louie made it himself, in a big silver bowl
at the back of the store, and he told us
he made it with snow shipped from Italy.

The junk man waved as he got to the corner,
taking his jingle and clip-clop toward 21st Ave,
his face so serious in the golden light.
When he tipped his hat, sparks flew through us,
as we stopped at the corner to call out goodbye,
made us suddenly want to jump Double Dutch,
or play tag in a wild stampede over fences,
and through the network of small back yards.

On those days we wanted to stay out forever.
The rust and the clutter, the feathers, the moving
machine parts, the slack leather reins in the junkman's
powerful big knuckled hands, the spots on the horse's back
where the hair had rubbed off, the plod and the footfall,
lingered in our heads, so we laughed out loud
in our beds, before falling asleep, convinced
that would be the only junk in our lives.

Milk

Celestial bottles on our daily kitchen table,
cloud white, delivered while we were sleeping,
to a metal box on the porch, and waiting to bless us
every morning; little popes in cream-colored hats.

Delicious cream, fog thick. Your choice: either shake
and mix it in, or eat it straight from the bottle with a spoon.
In winter they sometimes froze, cream pushing the caps up,
the way Jesus did the burial stone — rising, all ashimmer.

Real milk.

Not that crap in the can my grandparents used,
with its awful caramel taste. *Starvation artists;*
never got over *The Great Depression*, my mother said,
which made us notice how bony they were, the ridges in
their fingernails, as they punctured the can with an ice pick,
the way they never spoke to each other directly,
the hunch of their tired shoulders over supper.

Evaporated. Ugh, my father shivered.
Ruins the coffee: drip coffee they were proud of,
Eight O'Clock, from A&P, a deep brown that turned milky beige,
reminding them every day that their lives were on a different track,
pouring out like that white elixir, shoring them and their bones up
for retirement. Yeah, their kids would be bigger and stronger,
with legs thick as tree trunks. Because they spared no expense,
giving us all the milk we wanted at every meal.

Whole milk.

And how gladly we guzzled it, with or without talk at dinner,
washing down peas and pork chops, mornings drizzling it
over oatmeal, slowing down time as we skated on rivers of white,
as our parents gossiped about the neighbors before work.

At school, we looked forward to ten o'clock,
to getting our little half pint and a straw.
Milk worked its sacred arithmetic, fat
with pleasure, like an after-dinner cigarette.

Nobody thought about arteries then,
nobody worried about cancer.
We were in the pink, as they say,
washing each day down
with a creamy sense of amplitude,
all the dutiful soldiers, now home from the front,
drinking this measure of whiteness,
quiet as new fallen snow, teeth
clicking against the glass.

Crows

1.
All business,
they line the roadways,
the way the ushers used to
darken the back of the church
in their shiny black suits,
shifting from foot to foot
until the organ's raucous voice
announced it was time
to swoop in and catch
our meager generosities
in their soggy envelopes,
which we dropped like bits
of day old bread
into the long necked
baskets they slid
in front of us.

2.
When they lift all at once
their wings fill our heads
with the dark snap and billow
of the young priest's cassock,
when we stood at the classroom
window watching the wind
catch and whip it against
his legs like a sail,
holding him back with
invisible hands
as he hurried across
the playground
on his way to
give some poor
soul Extreme Unction.

3.
They waited in night's
big silence, like so many
folded signal flags,
to cast a veil of shadow
across our play.

Mary Coates

the only other Irish girl
at St. Anthony's, she had
porcelain freckled skin,
like a forest floor dappled
with leaf shadows,
and eyes, blue and clear
as the day she told me
what the f-word meant,
putting me out of my
ignorant misery with an
earthquake of forbidden
words that sent me
reeling away from her.

I wandered out in the open
with the smell of burning
cartons of milk all around me,
no longer at ease, and groaning
down dark corridors, standing
against brick walls all alone
with that terrible knowledge.

Mary Coates became a flasher
in a trench coat, stalking me
detective cool. She was
clearly out of my league.
I made sure we never
got a chance to talk again.

Confirmation

Girls dressed like brides,
carrying our brand new missals
into the pews, fingering our
rosary beads, red for the
tongues of fire at Pentecost,
red as the first drop of blood
on white cotton underpants.

Girls sitting ramrod straight,
awaiting the Bishop's questions,
prepared to spit back answers
we'd worked on for months, aching to be
counted among the anointed,
to have an invisible cross inscribed
on our foreheads, to kneel for
the little slap across the cheek
that said: *Eve's daughter,*
soft skinned seducer,
teeth sinking into forbidden fruit,
body awakening to the world.

Soon we would go boy crazy,
starting with long haired Jesus,
lying nearly naked under glass,
and taking us through Beatlemania,
and beyond, to the summer of love.

Dominic Savio

an altar boy
(A boy. If only she were a boy)
who levitated one day
in the quiet of the sacristy,
that's what the Sisters told them all:
kneeling in its golden light
and lifted by the angels
who loved his prayers.

Not you, the nuns always laughed
when she asked. No, *you're too
chubby. Your poor little prayers
would never get you off the ground.*

Don't get too big for your britches,
their wagging fingers cautioned,
but for her it was too late.

Holy pictures had already
become stories, and stories
boiled over with desire,
desire solidified, spilled
and slithered through the garden,
coiled around the branches of her heart.

Boys And Girls : The Rules

Boys, like wolves, had a pack of friends.
Girls, like turtles, went solo, spent time with family.

Boys built funhouses down the cellar
full of spider webs and skeleton grabbers.
Then they charged a dime to let you down there.

Girls watched boys from the back porch, as they colored
or played with dolls, until the baby had to be changed,
or fed in the shade of the peach tree in the yard.

Boys disappeared every day. They played stickball, rode their
bikes in the street, and sledded through intersections.
Their only job was to take out the garbage.

Girls helped their mothers shell peas, and peel carrots. They
couldn't ride bikes because they might get hit by a car. Besides,
there was so much wash to hang out. And diapers needed folding.

Like a Scrub Pine

he seemed to need so little,
his spare frame bent
on learning to play guitar,
my middle brother,
weathered and sturdy as a pilot boat
lost in the salt mist of music.

Years I watched him,
cheered for him, trying to green
and grow while a hurricane
raged between our parents,
until he shut himself away
from all of us, taking the knob
off the door to his room,
replying to our entreaties
with bouts of silence.

Now his solos take me back
to when he was four years old,
lying in the shade of the hedges,
and kicking his square sneakered feet,
as the two of us gobbled the huge
peaches I picked from our puny tree,
his little hands full of sweetness,
the sky blue and cloudless as his eyes.

Hunger Report #10

Walking home from school
up 20th Avenue I liked to
stop at Tommy Alois's store
to buy a Ring Ding whenever I could.

I remember the smell of meat,
and shuffling through the sawdust,
as Tommy stood behind the butcher block
in a white smock smeared with red.

And the dread I felt watching him clench
his sausage fingers and clear his throat
as I glanced sidelong at the knives,
and the head-sized knuckles of bone through the slanted glass,

the way my face had to harden like a mask
as I pretended I didn't hear his little jibes
about my mother's unpaid bill,
and handed over the dime I'd managed to sneak
out of her purse. She was never up in the morning when I left.

I opened it as fast as I could,
loving the way its little chocolate coat split
with a tiny snap under my teeth.
I remember the sneer on Tommy's face,

the taste of it mingled with devil's food cake,
and passing away in a slow dissolve
as I turned my back on him,
and made for the heavy door.

Fig

Old Mr. Farigna
across the street
never spoke to us,
but his fig tree did.

Augusts,
we wandered past his yard
to get a whiff of her
burgeoning incense, to eye
the promise of green globes
growing toward purple,
imagine them flowering on the inside,
their blooming taste of Paradise.

Autumns,
we watched him bend
those fragrant, green-handed
branches upwards, tying them tight
with clothesline, trussing her
like a prisoner smothered in plastic,
turning fullness into obelisk
with a final ragged coat of used linoleum.

There are bitter forces afoot, she said.
One needs plenty of protection.
Then, once the storms blow over, you can
lose the armor, and spread your wings.

The Circus Comes To Paterson

Once they set up Clyde Beatty's Big Top
at the foot of Sandy Hill, in the empty lot
where Teshon Village spread, in long barracks rows,
housing the soldiers and their wives after the war,
and then struggling families like ours,
until they finally knocked them down,
flattened them like furrows
ploughed up for just a few seasons
to give us all a chance to sow a future.

And there it was: our future,
in a house, with an alleyway and a garden,
on Summer Street, ripeness setting in, I guess,
because when the circus came
our parents were giddy too,
as we joined the crowd in the bleachers,
sitting in the backs of flat beds,
and pulled in a circle
like a wagon train at chow time.

And we were just like pioneers sitting there,
doing something we'd never done,
a circus right in our living room,
that's what it felt like
until the elephants came out
and no more than five minutes into the act
one of them broke ranks,
dragging the trainer with her,
the poor guy dangling like an earring
from the hook he held to the side of her head.

That elephant's berserk!, someone screamed,
and we screamed too when she charged at the trucks,
as people fled up the seats and dropped off the back.
We were paralyzed, which turned out to be all right

because she wasn't interested in us at all,
she was more intent on the freedom she saw
through an opening in the canvas
and was gone before we had that figured out.

The rest is hearsay.
Stories about her lurking behind the drugstore
so that Doc nearly had a heart attack
when he went to see why his dog was barking,
of how she wedged herself between
the shoemaker's house and garage
bending the aluminum as she eased her way back out,
how she reared up and stamped a footprint in the sidewalk,
before turning tail and running past our house
so Ralph next door thought he was going crazy
when he looked up from the paper
as she flew by like a bat out of hell.

They caught her way up high on the hill,
locked her in the back of a tractor trailer,
but the circus that day was done for,
there was no going back.
They worked her too hard, my mother said
to my Dad, *this is what happens*.

Meanwhile I stroked the garage's new curved edges
where her anger had made its mark,
watching the girls take turns
stamping the sidewalk as hard as they could
inside the ring of her footprint.

Columbia

wouldn't take the end of the rope,
to turn for Double Dutch,
so I could do some jumping too.

Yelled at me till I slapped her,
hard in the face to get her to stop.

Ran home to tell her mother,
who came flying down the alleyway,
to wag a finger at me, and say I should
pick on someone my own size,

I said, *come on! Who's kidding who?*.
Columbia was younger than me,
but she was as big as a horse!

This sent her mother reeling,
made her bee-line it to my house,
to make sure my mother knew
I'd called her daughter a whore.

Which struck me funny because
so much of the time, the mothers
and fathers called their daughters
putana instead of their names.

I didn't like her much to begin with,
but after that, she had permanent cooties.

Santa And Rosa

The girls next door
tricked me into eating rabbit
in a chicken cacciatore, then laughed
and laughed when I saw the toothy
little skull on their father's plate.

I watched them empty the sink,
so the fish that had been swimming there,
would slowly suffocate,
and pull a pigeon out of its cage,
after feeding it all day,
to twist its neck for soup,
with strong kitchen hands.

They thought it was funny
when I wouldn't stay
for dinner either time,
choosing to climb the fence
back to my house for macaroni
and cheese, or the blessed
ambiguity of meatloaf.

A gasping fish still
swam in my head,
its wide fins, its dark
singleness of purpose
all in vain, against
the white sink.
a pigeon kept eating
its way to a fatal
plumpness, as it trilled
in the cave of my chest.

Confessions

Bless me Father for I have sinned

1.
Sister Catherine told us stories
about martyrs every Wednesday,
how little children in China
were being tortured for loving Jesus,
the Communists giving them all
free passes to Heaven
on the ends of bayonets.

This made us think about how little
we have to suffer, so when we went
to light a candle after school,
I said a prayer and then I dipped
my fingers into the melted wax,
and offered up the burning as a sacrifice.

It really hurt, but I pursed my lips
and blew as hard as I could
until the wax clung to my fingers
like a pure white second skin.
It tasted of honey and crayons,
when I peeled it off and chewed it,
or those red lips you buy at the candy store.

Maybe suffering ahead of time
could help me later on, when I got to
commiting mortal sins, though I try
to do everything right. It would be
like a savings bond I could cash
when times were tight.

2.
On Good Friday we sat in silence
for three hours, in front of the glass
display case, where the ladies
laid Jesus's naked body out with
a white cloth strategically draped
across His holy parts.

I pretended I was Veronica,
the closest thing Jesus had
to a special fan. I mean didn't He
leave her a dreamy picture of His face?

The pew was so hard I couldn't seem to
sit still, and the quiet made me remember
the time I peeked through the bathroom
keyhole at my father, as he dried off,
the shock of it totally cured me of
ever wanting to spy again. and here
I was thinking *Jesus, not you too!*

3.
Last week, I was saying my penance,
and Marty from the newsstand
went into the confessional,
and talked so loud I heard
every one of his sins.
Every one.

I'm not crazy about Annette.
She hollers at me for the way
I moon over the comics
without buying one.
But I do that so I don't see
The National Enquirer:
headlines like *Chinese Lady Ate
Her Baby*, because they make me sick.

Marty's sins made me a little sick too.
I don't think he should have
done what he did to his wife.
I thought he was nice, since he lets us
have a soda once in a while,
but I was wrong,
and if I tell, I know that
I'll be committing a sin.
That's what Sister Mary said,
after my brother laughed when
Mrs. DeCarlo let a loud one go
on the way up to communion.

4.

I whisper swore at Sister Joanne,
and her Littlest Angels Club.
She said it was for girls who have vocations
but when I told her I thought I had a vocation,
she laughed and said I'd never get accepted
to be a sister the way I dress. *Where is the belt
to your uniform, Miss? And why doesn't your
mother bother to braid your hair?*

The girls all had cupcakes that looked like angels.
I think maybe, I'll be a missionary sister, since
people living in shacks wouldn't care about neatness.
Or maybe I'll grow up and get to clean the church;
be one of those ladies who dress the Infant of Prague.
He's so cute, with his crown and rosy kissable cheeks.
I wonder if He's sad that no one ever holds Him.
Maybe someday I'll be the one who gets to hold Him.

Nun Lore

They are bald beneath their wimples,
and their breasts shrivel up and fall off
when they take their vows.
Their convents have no mirrors,
and they have to dress in the dark.
They bathe only twice a week, and
they do it under white sheets
because looking at your own body,
if you belong to Jesus, is a sin.
They play baby whenever they can
with the Infant of Prague, and they fight
over who gets to dress Him. They have a big
crush on the near naked statue of J. they
lay out on Good Friday, but they know
nothing about sex, since their parents
gave them to the convent before
they could find any of that stuff out.
They think a miscarriage is an out of
control baby carriage rolling downhill,
that sitting on a boy's lap can get you
pregnant, unless you put a telephone
book on the boy's lap first, if you're
ever forced to double up in a car.
They love pizza and sometimes they
drink beer, and when they're drunk they
sing the Ave Maria until they cry.
Once a week they hold a rosary race,
and the one who is the fastest
gets a whole cake to herself.
They sleep in big drawers that pull
out of the wall, and they pretend
they're going to die every single night.

Warp and Weft

Five Years Old

and perched on the step-on
garbage can in the kitchen,
trembling,
as their argument
gets louder and louder.

Seeing the two of them
rise from the couch
red faced, arms flailing,
was worse than fireworks
spinning out of control
on the Fourth of July.

Each outburst startled me
into crying harder, as they
slapped and pushed and pulled,
across the coffee table between them.
Until, like an after burst, I woke
them out of gridlock.

They tried to pretend
they'd been merely *playing*.
But my mother's arms,
picking me up, were
shaking as hard as I was.
Dad wrapped himself around
her, holding the both of us close,
The two of them gentle again,
coaxing me into silence,
with smiles, frozen in place,
and full of big teeth.

Tex

had a bottle of cognac three feet tall,
kept it on the kitchen table
in a tilting contraption
so that he could easily pour it.
He used it for mouthwash every morning,
before he cooked three eggs
and six strips of bacon for breakfast.
I used to love to watch him
cover the yolks with pepper
until they were black,
and eat them in the big armchair
where he sat in his underwear watching TV.
Tex had ladies on his legs
and a ring tattooed around his finger,
ladies looking out at me from his upper arms,
wearing wooly bathing suits
and stockings knotted on tilting chubby legs.
He always said that he hated them,
tried to burn one off with acid once
but it hurt too goddamned much to do them all.
When he laughed his gold tooth brought
the light right there to his mouth,
as if he were speaking sunlight.
He was foreman of the Foundry
at Wright's Aeronautical, but he
said he worked in Hell itself.
Before he married Nana, we assumed
he chased rustlers too, catching them
and hauling them to the hoosegow.
The way he must have gotten his cowboy
name because when Mommy ran away
from home, and took us to live in a rooming
house, it was Tex who told Daddy he'd knock
him on his ass, if he ever touched her again.

Turtle Girl

hides in the heavy carapace
as her parents sharpen
their teeth on one another,
a chaos of quicksilver portents,
always rippling through
their watery rooms
like shimmering carp.

She watches, still as the eye
of the hurricane, barely
moving, so much slower
than the whirl and
wheedle of brothers.

She pulls in and waits.
She is patience itself,
a green hope that grows
bigger every year.

Somewhere a better future
is moving toward her
one sluggish step at a time.

Water Office

I learned the water office
by washing dishes
every night after supper.
There were always so many of them,
food caked, grease smeared,
they seemed to tower over me
waiting to be held
beneath the warm fall of the water
I imagined I was the Baptist,
easing them into a clean place one by one.

My mother was my bishop in this.
Her most important lesson:
that they'd be there in the morning,
ice cold and smelling sour
if I left them to their own devices
that they'd be there tomorrow and tomorrow
and the next day, in endless porcelain waves.

This rise and fall of dishes in so much need:
the litany of a woman's life.
Especially if she's lucky enough
to be ordained a mother and wife.

The Hunger Angels

first came to her when they were fighting.
It was as if the little girl had put her ear to a seashell.

They showed her how her father swallowed his anger.
They swirled inside his undertow of loneliness,
swam in his beer, made fun of the white heron poses,
he learned as a boy in a kitchen
where there was never enough to eat.

And she watched them light as hummingbirds
as they buzzed her mother's fork, oozed out of her sandwiches.

When Mommy was quiet they gathered in her hair
stirring up the racket of memory with its abuses, desertions,
the hard work that made her disappear into cooking pots,
and gourmet magazines full of creamy sauces.

She watched the two of them
tangle with one another in despair.
She wondered how the angels multiplied so quickly,
why they all had her parents' faces in miniature.

Put us in your hope chest, they said,
when she was eight years old.
Someday you'll open it and we'll have grown,
like dumplings or loaves of bread.
No head of a pin for us, babe.
We'll keep you fidgety company.
Just fire up those cravings.

In her innocence she welcomed them,
glad to be included, not knowing
how else the story might have gone.

We Learn About Love

from the stories our parents tell at the supper table,
like sober news commentators creating history
they begin with an axiom: *It doesn't pay to be grabby,*
they say. *Take Tessie around the corner.*

Tessie ran the local grocery for her parents.
She was what we all called homely:
short and brown and thick as a little fireplug.

But Tessie had a beautiful husband,
her father had imported for her from Italy.
And she glowed when she had to talk for him
to the rest of us, which she did because he didn't speak English.

Day after day he went off to who knows what job or where,
with his black wavy hair, white teeth, and permanent tan.
But, let's face it: what he said and did wasn't important.
*What was, was that he was Tessie's, and that the women
said three Hail Marys whenever he passed them.*

Until one summer this angel went up on the roof to fix it,
and in a grab at a sliding hammer plunged
to the sidewalk and broke his neck.
Just like that! My mother snapped her fingers,
her whole life gone in a heartbeat!

Tessie must have been shattered,
but two days after the funeral she was back,
shuffling around the store in her mules and peds,
using the claw to grab the heavy cans off the shelves,
dropping them down and catching them in one hand,
like she'd always done. But it wasn't the same.
It used to be fun to go in there, to watch her dance

with the mop, or sing to the baskets of fava beans.
Now the store seemed more like Pompeii, what
with Tessie buried alive every night in its ashes.

It's a shame, my mother sighed, as she got up to clear the table.
You go after too much, and you're in for nothing but heartache.
Yup, my father said, as he lit a cigarette, *it doesn't pay to kid yourself.*
My brother and I chewed on this and swallowed,
eyeing each other through a growing cloud of smoke.

Dee Dee And Pop Pop

She matched him, my mother said.
Oh, she was his match, his lucifer,
each drink he belted down
she'd cough back up,
spitting into Kleenex
what had set good fire
to his throat and belly.

Each battle with pneumonia
like a month long binge,
him wondering if he'd
ever get her home again.

Oh, butter wouldn't melt
in her mouth, my mother said.
Day after day, no words
passing her lips, except for
the constant hiss of Hail Marys.

The clear walls of the oxygen tent
between them, deceptively
cool to his touch.

Sleeping Beauty

Like a frog out of the water,
like a big clumsy fly
caught in a screen,
I entered womanhood
flailing my long legs.

Jumping Double Dutch, in sneakered feet
pounding a Morse Code of denial
into the sidewalk, so it echoed
throughout the neighborhood.

Not me, it said, *not me,*
I'll play with dolls forever,
I'll be a boy if I want to,
I'll go off and play by the railroad tracks.

Or spinning crazy like a top
in the grass of the backyard,
almost mowing mother's roses down with my arms,
then swooning beneath our peach tree
heavy with ripe fruit.

Dizzy, it always made me dizzy,
and sleepy too, this newly tilting
pigeon thrumming inside me.

Thought I'd never want a prince
bending over me —his face
so much like a brother's
with its teasing eyes
and mouth that kisses too hard.

Hardware

Jean Scalvino used to cover her round breasts
with an apron and sweep the sidewalk every day.
But the store she owned with her brother stayed dark and murky,
its hardware hung from the ceiling: coffee pots and ladles,
scrub boards and galvanized buckets, ivory cups
and dish mops, all the tools, the apparatus of housework,
waiting to be adopted, and wrapped in newspaper.

You watched her hands as she swaddled
the piggy bank you bought, and crossed it with string.
Her fingers had bulbs on the end like wild onions,
her fingers, her whole body curled this way and that,
crabbed and frayed as an old scrub brush.
And you were the witness, as the work she did
turned her into what she sold. You saw
the hook that beckoned her to her rest.

Phoebe

Took in ironing, the air in her kitchen
starchy as the taste of Communion.
Her clouds of cottony steam
haloed neighbors who came and went,
with their bundles of chaos,
their tidy packets of hangers.

She was their Queen for a Day,
her scepter, the soda bottle sprinkler,
sitting on a fridge full of damp white
shirts rolled in plastic bags. She had
the cleanest windows on the block.
She liked to scrub and wax her
floors by the white moon
glow of Million Dollar Movie.

She inspired the other women,
gave them direction, you might say,
in an otherwise long and aimless
stream of their post-war layoff lives,
so they scrubbed and polished
as if they were contestants
in some enormous game show.

But it didn't sustain them.
Unhappiness rolled over all of us
big as a mushroom cloud. It tainted
our innocence, made them irritable
and absent-minded much of the time.
Some of their marriages suffered,
until one by one, they felt they
just had to go back to work,
to make ends meet, or to save up
for a move to a better neighborhood.

Uncle Charlie

How I wished he would
some day marry me,
his unconditional love
like a road I wanted
to run down, white carpeted,
dotted with bows and vigil lights
that burned like a heart on fire.

I was four years old
walking down the aisle,
while he, black-tuxedoed,
waited at the end for his bride,
my eyes full of him, and only him,
as I scattered handfuls of petals
pink as my cheeks along the way,
till my mother pulled me into
the big front pew, and Aunt Jeanne,
all in white floated into view.

Uncle Joe

When he smiled
there was always
a glob of brown tobacco
on his front teeth.

When he leaned back,
and scratched his beer belly
the smell of sweat and gin mill
clouded out into the room.

The aunts and my mother
would shake their heads,
and wrinkle their noses,
chanting his list of offences:

how in the yellow
light of an afternoon
he drove his father's car
through Scalvino's fence,
then sat there so tanked up
he couldn't move
like the family's dirty linen
laid out for all the neighbors,

or the dark day he staggered into
his mother's bedroom,
opened her dresser drawer
and peed all over her neatly folded personals,

how he ate leftover spaghetti
by the handful from the icebox,
standing and smacking his lips
in the blue glare of the midnight kitchen.

Even at birth, he'd been mud
in his father's eyes, being sickly
and taking all his mother's attention.

There seemed to be no end to the trouble
he could cause the family,
so that even we nieces and nephews
took to rolling our eyes
whenever we saw him.

I mulled him over for years,
this blight on the Daly name
who must have been sent
to us for a reason.

Maybe he was like
the boils of Job
sent by God to test us.
After all, God sent angels
disguised as beggars, didn't he?
To measure people's hearts?

If Uncle Joe was a test,
I figured the family
grade was pretty low
because Uncle Joe never
laughed without somehow
hurting himself,
and crying a little bit too.

Silk Mill Sopranos

They called the women,
who worked in the Paterson mills,
silk mill sopranos.

Transformed at fourteen
from school girls into pickers, winders,
and warpers, great wooden bobbins
spinning a raucous incessant din.
Shouting over the clack of the looms
in rooms thick with flurries of cotton snow,
taking cigarette breaks to ease their itchy lungs.

No need to be lady-like in Paterson,
they told us. Not when you can pay
the bills yourself, not when your
bathtub ginned through the Roaring Twenties,
and lived through the Great Depression,
not when you can make yourself heard
from at least two blocks away.

What else is there to say, about women
who rushed a growler of beer home for each day's
supper, to insure they'd forget the constant
ache in their legs, who swore like sailors
in several languages, and laughed so hard,
sometimes, they wet their pants, patterns of silk
jacquard dancing for a lifetime in their heads?

Nana's Blue Jay Sisters

pecking at her, pecking at her,
their silk mill soprano voices
accusing and raucous.

Just like Pa's, when he cocked
his head and made the *crow eyes*,
laughed a bitter laugh
and called her *Big Face*.

Hollanders hate a *show off*.

Nana all dimples and mischief,
a baby, attached to Mama,
pretending to be the good girl,
with a circle of boys around her.

Empty wagons, they said.
Always noisy.

Aunt Lou, Aunt Chris, Aunt Marie.
Nana wrapped in a cloud of their glee,
as they sat at the bar on Straight St.
trying to get a rise out of her.

Too much like the Tantes, their namesakes,
who landed the flock in Paterson, and burned
their wooden shoes in the kitchen stove.

Elsie's sharp-tongued sisters eating crow,
and doing a barefoot hootch dance
around the sheets from her wedding bed.

Two big flapping wings
pinned onto the clothesline,
shimmering like the Zuiderzee,
one flecked with archipelagos of red
while Nana grew pink cheeked
and bowed her head.

Mouse Pie

was what they fed to bed wetters years ago to get them to stop
or better yet, fried mice on a stick,
which surely must have spawned enough
insomnia to seem like a cure.

That's why, I mutter to myself,
my head nodding up and down
above the book in my lap
so full of homely bits of sadism like this,

that's why we were overrun with mice when we lived in the projects.
The slaps on the butt hadn't worked any better
than the dry cell buzzer that never did go off
when the pee soaked through to the rubber pad underneath.

Nothing worked until the mice came flooding in
on the humid waves of my mother's anger, so many
they made nests in the couch and darted
back and forth as we watched TV,
So many that we cooked them in the stove more than once,

and their terrible bacony smell filled the house
with a purgatorial futility that fogged around us for years.
Now I understand what I felt but could never see:
that her accidental suppers were meant for me.

Rough Cut

Ma was drawn to divorcees,
who lived on their own, and took her
carousing. Women who skanked around
in bars filled with men, who shimmied
to tunes on the jukebox, and flirted themselves
into some fella's arms. Women who swore
like sailors, and, like her, had it pretty rough,
who had to work to make ends meet, though
the ends seldom did. Women who had
eight kids, and a husband who drank, daughters
who ran away because they were pregnant.

These women were part of her
secret life, away from us, the happy
hours when she could pretend she was free,
and full of adventure, not trapped in a place
where she struggled to get through each day.

They polished her nails and made her up.
She drove them to pick up groceries.
They baked her pies to thank her
for giving their kids our *extra* toys.
She asked them to babysit, so she
could go shopping in peace.

Mostly they invited her out.
Another girls' night, she'd say,
with a smile. Completely harmless.
But these girls were wild.
They were rough cut, no strangers
to trouble. And though it wasn't
obvious, Ma was just the same.

The House They Bought
On Summer Street

grew ripe and fetid as an old peach
let go of by the tree with a terrible thud.

Too heavy it was, even for Summer Street,
sugar pleasing no one but the flies,
what sweetness, there had been, gone to vinegar
all swollen and oozy with lies.

*****

A woman who sleeps
on the living room couch
every night, and again before work,
can bring herself to do nothing
but tear things apart.

Curtains come down and windows
don't get done, paneling's bought,
but never put up, though she took off
the old stuff a long time ago, leaving
behind a swirly crust of adhesive.

When the pipes burst in
the bathroom it was all she
could do to get the plumber in.
The walls can wait till Hell freezes over,
she hissed and meant it.

Hell like the toilet upstairs,
which hadn't been flushed
since they moved in;
its throat clogged
with ugly secrets

Her anger is so big
she can no longer talk.

She cleans a place at the table
and puts on make-up,
gets lost in the glide of her
lipstick and disappears.

*****

A man sits in his boxer shorts at the kitchen table
smearing blue cheese onto Ritz crackers as his daughter watches.
His legs are long and so white
you can see his veins
snaking blue underneath.

His chest is white like that too,
in fact he seems to be wearing a negative shirt
limned by the brown of his arms and neck and head,
a shirt bought working construction and sewn by the sun.

The kitchen is full of the smell of sweat
and beer and feet too long in shoes
as he eats his little snack,
unaware, in his funk, of the girl until she speaks,
toeing the floor her eyes all asparkle.
Can I have some? She asks,
determined to take what she can, blue or not.

*****

A boy works on a go-cart in the back yard.
Anything, anything with wheels that will take him away.
He plays down by the railroad tracks with his friends,
and they talk, chests all puffed out, about some day
hopping a freight. He hides whenever he sees his father
staggering down the street. He cries whenever

his mother tries to sit him down to talk.
He torments their two little brothers
by telling them there's a wolf
in the vacuum cleaner,
but they aren't fooled.
They know that he is the wolf.

*****

Shame clings to them like a scab that doesn't heal.
It sleeps in the big walk-in closet among the un-ironed
shirts, it curls like a snake on the floor, such
a jumble of ironing, you can't tell any more
what fits them from what doesn't.

The girl knows how to sprinkle water over
cotton before she irons it, roll a shirt up tight,
and put it into the fridge overnight, to make
sure it's wrinkle-free in the end.
But there are too many shirts, they've spilled
out of the basket, until she's afraid
she'll drown if she goes too near them.

She feeds shame to the baby in spoonfuls
along with his applesauce, it speaks
a language of rough handling
and resentment that has to escape
from her mouth, from her hands,
it eats away the skin on her feet
when water gets in through the holes
in her shoes she's made from walking
and walking and jumping rope with wild abandon.
She cuts a milk carton into the shape of an insole
and wonders where she'll wander off to next.

*****

It's her job to hang clothes out every day on the line,
arranging them all like this: mother's flannel nightgowns
and black waitress uniforms, father's heavy work shirts,
his dark green pants a forest of legs, brothers' dungarees
in three graduated sizes, all with holes in the knees,
their socks that even bleach can't make white again.

She hangs them by the toes, the hems, the legs,
joins them together with tight wooden pegs,
the pulley squeaking time as she reels them
out as far as they can go, so the wind puffs them
up, big as udders ready for milking, move to
the music that she hears, grow giddy drinking air in
great big gulps. It's a party and she's the hostess, as
one by one they ask her to dance, and her answer is always yes.

Blessing of the Throats

Through the intercession of St. Blaise
may God deliver us from all evils of the throat
and from every other evil

I hurried up the steps of the church
to kneel at the altar rail,
as the Bishop stood inside it,
gold and ivory as Benediction itself,
his crossed candles cutting
the incense-thick air.

He blessed the others,
then lightly touched my neck too,
with the candles, the golden cord
that held them binding us all together.

I remember his hands,
smooth and waxen as he traced,
the icy crosses slick with Chrism.
I remember the hum of the blessing,
and wanting the Bishop to be St. Blaise,
to set me free from what choked me.

There would be drops of red on the stones
as I coughed it all up like a tide of glass,

like a tiny wing giving way, that finally opens.

What silenced me would be called forth: the fights,
my father staggering up the stairs to sleep alone,
the hiss of my mother's rage swallowing my rage,
her nights with other men tracing
a slivered path with no outlet.

I wanted to tell him a burning tongue

would rise above me, if only he could release it.
But he moved away, a wraith in a long cape,
dumb to the flightless girl kneeling there,
too shy to break the silence.

Auntie Ee

always showed up
with a coloring book and crayons
once I could sit up in bed,
with measles, mumps, chicken pox,
glaring at her through sunglasses,
or baking in a crust of calamine,
as she coolly pulled out burnt sienna
or umber for the wings of the owl
sitting between us.

I watched her nod
as Mother told her
what a horror I'd been:
gagging on the medicine she gave me,
throwing its cherry awfulness up
all over the bathroom,
leaving the two of us
speckled from head to toe.

Then she winked at me and said
those medicines gagged her too.
I was sensitive, and my mother should
just give up on my being a trooper.

One Christmas she gave me a doll
that had three faces I could spin
around at will, one of which was fixed
in an open-mouthed cry.

She called me Little Iodine,
and chuckled whenever
I sassed the other grown-ups,
saying the apple hadn't
dropped far from the tree.

This scrappy aunt, who could never
have kids of her own, and so
took me under her wing,
coaching me toward
a defiant fall from grace,
that eventually led me
into a life of my own.

Aunt Mary

I remember picking
armfuls of spiral-leafed
branches, with my cousin Carol.
Bright red bunches of feathers,
we dragged across the lawn
to adorn her plain little house.

How she caught fire when she
saw them, screamed they were
poison sumac.
Ordered us to turn around
and take them back
where we'd found them.

After my mother got the phone call
about Carol covered from head to toe
in running sores, I waited
for them to erupt on my skin too,
but nothing happened.

It was the first time I felt invulnerable.
Something had entered my life:
the miracle of wine red leaves,
the miracle of fire that didn't
burn. Sumac choosing me
because I looked beyond
its poison, saw beautiful,
and wanted to bear witness.

Red

Nana loved to go out on the town.
She wore midnight blue taffeta that whispered
innuendoes as she walked, in dainty heels.
Her breath smelled like Apple Jack
and cigarettes. It sent me reeling
when she'd pull me close, to say how much
I owed my mother for bringing me
into this world, for the food I ate so much of,
for the Catholic education she begged the nuns for.

Over cake, she said I asked too many questions,
my mind was unquenchable. She pointed a wine red nail
at my feet which were too big. That's why I was so clumsy.
I took after my father. My face was long and sad like his,
not sweet and round like my mother's.

When she swept into our living room a darkness descended
over me like a hood, so I didn't know where I was any more,
had to echolocate by her gruff and growly voice,
its cross between Granny and wolf.

That is until I was thirteen or so, and sassing her
became my Confirmation, her slap at my face
like the one I got from the Bishop in church:
a wake up call out of girlhood. It was great.
She didn't speak to me for three whole years.

I stopped blushing, and let go of my fears,
developed a manifesto, made ready for
the blood gush I knew was on the horizon,
and grew taller than all the women in my family.
From a distance I watched her eye me, like a hunter
does his prey. But, like a fern reborn,
I uncurled anyway, ready to face the blade.

Sonia and Tamara

The Russian girls across the street,
wore leather jackets and black eyeliner.
They smoked cigarettes bought for them
by Tamara's brother Viktor. They played
cards every night with Sonia's sister Hanna.

At fifteen, I took to sneaking out every night,
telling Dad I was going up to bed, then climbing
out the window in my room, onto the upstairs porch
and down the stairs in stocking feet, racing across
Summer Street, to stay up till midnight playing
five hundred rummy. One winter night, I banged
my shin on a piece of protruding ice, and Sonia's
babushka'd mother made me a poultice of grated
potato and sugar to stop the swelling, which like
a miracle it did. One summer night I stood lookout
for the girls as they climbed behind the bushes
on Sandy Hill to make out with two random boys.

I kept this up until my brother checked my room
one night and found it empty. Dad had him
lock the upstairs door and window, so I had to
come in through the kitchen, and walk past him
sitting up waiting for me, the TV blaring.
I was shaking, shoes in hand, as I stood
in the living door, bracing for what he'd say.

But he'd fallen asleep after a couple of beers,
and stayed that way as I snuck back up to bed.
The next morning Dad demanded to know where
I'd been, and though I didn't know why, I insisted
I'd been in my room asleep all night, and I wouldn't,
couldn't back down. Like a dancing princess I was
desperate for adventure, and to his credit,
my father made peace with defeat.

Georgette

My mother's cousin was the only one
in the family to marry money.

Going to her house, with its magenta
bathroom fixtures, its brick fireplace
and curving sectional, its kidney shaped
pool, and house-sized cabana, was as good
as a trip to Coney Island. We marveled at
their laundry chute, the paneled basement
family room with its pool table and bar,
the slide that whipped us into cool water bliss.

Georgette always stood at the kitchen counter,
ready to dish out Cokes and chips, and whatever
else we wanted, while her husband lounged
in the living room smoking cigars.

She had a good heart, my mother said,
whenever I complained about my cousin's
hand-me-down chubby clothes. They
smelled wrong, and never fit me right.
She gave us all of their old stuff, since they
were always getting new stuff; washers,
a bedroom set, a rotisserie oven, bicycles.
My dad would grit his teeth, and go get
whatever it was, in a borrowed pickup truck.

The way we lived was nowhere near as pretty.
Our house was half torn apart, the work never
finished, and haunted by random disaster.

Georgette may have been a sweetheart,
but her children made me sick. Each
perfect shiny thing they had, was
another thorn piercing me to the quick.

Sister Mary

skipped a few of us from
7th to 8th grade, on the first
day of school, without asking
our parents. I was 11 years old,
and struggling, having missed
a whole year of lessons, and
we had no money for tutors.

She made us recite our lessons aloud,
and carried around a pointer,
that could be slammed on the desk
to wake us up. She tapped it on
the floor as she walked between us.

Every Friday, she sat at her outsize
desk reading our grades aloud,
as we listened with folded arms,
our uniforms stuck to our chairs.

When she came to a failure,
her yellow smile grew bat wings,
and flew toward the culprit, hungry
for blood. DALY .... SIXTY!

It was a performance, her poison-honey
voice bringing on a wave of snickers,
from the others, catching me
in an undertow of despair.
Once I started crying, I couldn't stop.

It's the one time, my mother came to the rescue.
At the meeting they had, Sister Mary said
I wasn't as smart as the other teachers
made me out to be. My mother dismissed
that as nonsense, and said Sister Mary was

the one who'd failed, not me. She had us
transferred to St. Joseph's, so I could go
back into 7th grade, to learn the stuff I hadn't
yet learned. Soon, she said, Sister Mary would
fade, and I'd get back to the girl I used to be.

Women As Big As The World

My mother, and her mother bigger still, enveloping
me in the do's and don'ts, all the frowning
dimpled faces, and stocky bodies,
with stubby fingers wagging: *No.*

And my grandmother's mother before her,
wafting cabbage, and bacon grease perfume.
All the way back to Holland they go,
each generation more massive than the last.

Each of them cast from a similar mold,
drifting down, like bell jars,
clotting the air, a set of Russian Mama dolls,
round faced, and babushka'd in the rain,
arms folded over aprons, accepting life as pain,
and work, always work. Too busy to pull a child close.

O lineage of matriarchs, you tucked your sheets
too tight. My ears still sting from the judgements
you flung, my cheeks, from the slapping wheel
that chased me as I turned away. Your days
have passed. No more seeds locked in the pod, no more
embryos, in multiple wombs, who cannot fully be born.

The last thing I want to do is descend, like you did,
over my kids, to risk snuffing out their light.
I do not need, like you did, to always be right.

Smoke

It wasn't the rings
Uncle Charlie blew,
the way they came alive,
curling and growing over our heads,
reaching through the kitchen
soft as ghost lips, saying *Oh*.

It wasn't the clouds
that drifted through the air as we played,
or watched TV sitting on the floor,
the ones that billowed dragon-mighty
out of our mother's nostrils
even when she was telling us we'd been good.

Not Uncle Joe's famous,
Oh dear, a bottle of beer, a Woodbine, and a match,
which he said as he yawned and stretched,
heading out to the kitchen to empty the parlor ashtray, either.

*****

The dance of their hands is what I loved most.

The tan ballet of my father tapping the end of a filter-less *Pall Mall*
on a spot just below his knuckle bones
before putting it between his lips.
The barely perceptible thud of it,
full of Humphrey Bogart strut and confidence.

The jitterbug whip of Aunt Mary's
lanky fingers pulling a shred of tobacco
off the pink tip of her tongue, mid-sentence, the smooth
turn of her head as she reached for the lipstick-tinted *Lucky*
perched on the edge of her saucer, bringing it up
to her mouth to finish it off.

The manicured foxtrot that Nana did with Auntie Ee,
at our Sunday kitchen table stroking aside
the ashes in the tray, with the tip of a lit
Phillip Morris, straightening the whole thing
into careful little piles: neat as their kitchen cabinets.

The way window light caught the brown and yellow *Camel* stains
on Pop-Pop's slender fingers, as if he'd become tobacco itself.

*****

And the brown globs of spit mixed with tobacco leaf
on Uncle Joe's front teeth weren't enough to deter me
from starting up in college. Nor were the burns
from running into random lit ends,
as their hands quickly dropped, post-drag.
It always sent sparks flying,
and there was crying,
but not enough of it
to make a difference.

It wasn't the fact that the stories
about our constant mischief:
Tommy and I in our pajamas,
rolling around in the snow
with the satin comforter from their bed,
or spreading lipstick all over our arms and heads,
or dumping cornflakes and flour and syrup
on the floor outside the cupboard,
never really added up.

They were just our own little myths,
spread around us like halos,
auras we could take with us
along with the smoke into adulthood.
Until we found out

that Mommy had been leaving us
alone while she went down the block
to buy her *Salems*.

What a funny family.

*****

When Uncle Allen's little backache
turned into lung cancer, I went to live
with Aunt Aggie, to care for my cousins,
while she tended him in the hospital bed
and oxygen tent that dominated their little house.
The kids and I ate *Pop Tarts* in the kitchen,
and I went outside periodically,
smoked even at the funeral home,
joining two thirds of the family
down in the basement, shaking our heads,
and crying as we lit up. Aunt Aggie wasn't
even driving yet. How was she going
to get a job, let alone support three kids?
I'd had to sit up with Uncle Allen only once,
during the night, praying the whole time
that he wouldn't die while I was there alone with him.
His mouth was open wide
as he struggled for breath after breath.
A yawn that became everlasting.

*****

Now, almost twenty-five years after
my first child was born smoke-free,
I'm finally off my high horse,
and saying: What did we know?

We did just what they wanted us to.
We went to the movies; frowned with Edward R. Murrow

over the state of the world, swigged highballs with Dean Martin,
our voices, like Lucy's, a little huskier each year...

We wanted to feel anointed, smudged by all that smoke
as if it were incense; our lives a feature story in Life Magazine.

Smoking was not an addiction then.
People worked hard. They led clean lives, immaculate lives really,
and then sat down to inhale what they thought of as leisure,
or glamour, or the ruggedness we needed to keep going.
We wanted to be God's rat pack.

I saw a poet, not too long ago,
smoking a pack of *American Spirits*,
and she quickened me to these memories,
sensual and ethereal as the smoke I used to inhale.

We were just trying, weren't we,
to suck the souls we were losing back in
to the hollows around our hearts
where they belonged?

Goodbye House

Goodbye Dad. After too many
years of fighting over money,
over beer, over everything,
him hugging the four of us,
as we wept, and quickly closing
the front door behind him, to keep
the cold from creeping in.
It crept in anyway.

Goodbye mortgage money,
and hello clothes we needed.
Our mother decided the house
could go up for Sheriff's sale,
this house, full of small joys,
and too much heartache,
we'll be turning our backs on.

Goodbye house. We have to go
into our future, foggy though it be.
An apartment in Prospect Park
awaits us. We will take the bus
to our same old school.

Goodbye house. We'll never forget you,
and your blue stories. Our baby brother
drew one with a red peaked roof, and
the four of us standing beneath it. This is
where we live now most of the time.

Life is a riddle made of keyholes.
How quickly a key becomes
meaningless, once it loses its door.

On the Bus: N. Straight St.

All the clocks are stopped
in these neighborhoods,
we pass through. The city's
poorest -- left to fend
for themselves like
neglected children.

I feel invisible here,
No one notices me sitting
blank-faced and watchful.

Too much despair
to look at, creeping up to swallow
us – rising like the river
after heavy rain, a crooked
picture nobody bothers to put right.

A drunk walks down the street
past a one-legged woman who sits
statue still, staring into faces,
she'll never see again. He staggers
on, as I sit in my silence, knowing
he's lost like the rest of us, and holding
on to the shine as long as he can.

On the Bus: To the Indian Black Mustache

Forgive me, but ...
as you were leaving,
and looked back, I had
a rush of confidence,
and when our eyes met,
I must've lost my head ...
I'm sorry. I should've known
you were looking through me ...
It was foolish of me ...
I wasn't even happy,
and now I've gone
and hurt myself ...
I didn't mean to ...
smile.

On the Bus: Rebirth

It all works together.
A mob of purple irises
pushing against a wrought iron
fence, like commuters pressing
to get on board. Here, a heavy
bower of peach colored roses,
necklacing a shabby bungalow,
there a pot of begonias, lush,
and pinking a fire escape.

It all works together.
Everyone doing their small part,
to celebrate a late city spring.
A girl talks to the chalk drawings
she's making, to brighten the sidewalk,
Even the homeless contribute, sitting
down on a warm slate stoop in the sun,
their eyes small blooms of gratitude.

My Mother And My Father

at the kitchen table,
in a cloud of cigarette smoke,
unable to look each other in the eye.

Neither one moves much,
beyond the occasional lift of
hand to mouth, the draw of lips
on a filter tip, a tap on
the edge of the ashtray.

So two lives fill up;
ashes enough to paint
their faces on Jupiter,
cigarette butts that go on
to infinity, the two of them
spreading out, huge enough
to exhale galaxies.

They are caught in
their marriage bed's
gravity field, a black
hole holding them
in suspension,
swallowing all
the happiness
they tried to
slap together.

The stillness I witness,
like the night sky's,
is deceptive.

The forces of time and
history are moving
them, fast as comets,
toward early demise.
Soon they will be two
distant astral bodies
that call me into the dark.

There I Am In 1966

listening to the boys sing a cappella
in St. Joe's stairwell after school.
Crouching low in the dark, two flights above them
so they can't see they caress me with their voices:

A Smokey Robinson solo
drifts slow as incense around a girl
who rarely shows up for class any more,
a girl who needs a Miracle more than ever.

Then the Righteous Brothers accuse her
in harmonies so sweet, so filled with longing
and forgiveness, they cancel out the croaking
of the crab who teaches Algebra II, and the
cowboy nun who tells her she looks like a witch.

Here in this aerie, the fullness she feels, the certainty
that somewhere in her future a Soul Man waits,
cool and beautiful as Sam and Dave.
The Rascals reassure her: *Love is a beautiful thing,
so beautiful*, and she can almost believe them.

It lifts her, and she floats home, lingering
at every corner, bathing in the afterglow.
Until she turns from Market onto Summer Street
and sees two black girls coming toward her,
fast in their converse high-tops, on music as big and loud
as the bright combs sticking out of their hair.

They are listening to the Temptations
on a transistor radio and swinging their hips.
She can hear them singing: *You're so-o-o sweet,
you coulda been a piece of candy*,
owning it with their bodies and their voices,

and she wants to smile, say hello,
say it's her music too, start singing
and dancing right there on the sidewalk,
lusting for the beat, bathing in it,
showing them she's one of their own.

But as they draw near
fear spins a cyclone in her chest,
so she finds herself crossing the street instead,
trying her best to look like she has a reason.
But the two of them mistake her cowardice
for the kind of scorn they've bumped into
in this neighborhood too many times.

They stop and glare, fingers wagging in the air:
You better cross the street, Miss Cracker!
You don't want to get next to us,
cause we'll slap that little pink cheek
if you don't watch out!

Across the street a pudgy white girl stands
trying to look like she's suddenly heard her mother
calling her name, but she's not fooling anyone.
They burst into buckets of laughter.
Everyone knows that no one
is home for a girl like this.
Just a sink full of last night's dishes,
and a recipe for supper set out on the table.

Tomorrow she'll sleep and sleep until it's three o'clock,
dreaming those boy voices, like arms wrapped around her tight.
When she wakes, the bell will already be ringing, the other
students pouring out into the street in their uniforms,
exuberant to have their freedom back, facing
the prospect of after-school cookies baked
from scratch in Betty Crocker kitchens.

Sister Marietta

let us follow her down
the well of ourselves
to feast on the glistening
salmon of poetry.

She held the divining rod.

So what if I wrote about riding to nowhere,
or chewed away at my own thumbs
insisting they tasted good?

Sister Marietta helped me
weave a wishing cap
out of strings of words,
and blessed it with
the quickening of comets:
her "A's" crossing
the night sky of the page,
trailing little plusses
along behind them.

Poem for Dottie

We were the brainy girls,
the quiet girls, the nerdy girls,
who spent our lunch hours far away
from the popular kids, talking about
The Beatles, and Herman's Hermits,
writing poems like John Lennon's,
listening to Donovan and Bob Dylan,
singing to a pocket transistor radio.

We were the plain girls, the verbal girls
clowning around. Then editing the yearbook,
and the literary magazine, writing gossip
columns for the weekly school paper.

You were the girl with the editing pencil behind
her ear. I was the girl with the notebook of poems,
she took everywhere. Having brothers, we brooked
no boy nonsense, and wisecracked back until
they left us alone. Mr. Lorenzo said we were
gifted, but all together too serious.

When the yearbook came out, I'd been
absent so much, I'd become a sad-eyed mystery,
seen by others as merely Jolly. It was your attention,
and insistence, I do my share, that kept me from
completely flunking out, for which I am grateful.

The ironic girls, the sarcastic girls, how we joked
away our unhappiness, the depression our mothers
sunk into, leaving us both to fend for ourselves.
But when we sang Second Hand Rose, on Class Night,
we became the hilarious girls, the zany girls, like Lucy
and Ethel, bound for glory and adventure. Afraid of nothing.

Senior Year

The boys had a game they played, every
Friday afternoon during Chemistry class.

One whistled low, while another hissed
out a name, and then slowly they'd all
edge backwards, or forwards,
or sideways, in their desks,
homing in on the chosen one,

reaching under him from all sides,
like they would a hen,
to collect her eggs,
only they were grabbing
at body parts instead,
all the roundnesses
that make a boy vulnerable.

And the boy tried what he could,
to evade the pain of the squeeze,
until desk after desk
came crashing down in a heap,
and Sister Robert Jeannette
jumped up on her chair,
like a two year old having a tantrum.

By the time the principal got there,
it was over, and of course we all denied it,
even in the face of detention,
looking so stunned and hurt and studious,
that the poor nun often backed down,
throwing up her hands, and saying, *never mind*.
After all it had happened so fast, it was more like a dream.

We girls were in awe of these terrible maneuvers
and not a little afraid of what they could cook

up next, if the spirit moved them.
And so chose to ignore them in the halls,
were suddenly too busy, talking to each other,
about ironing our hair, or pale pink lipstick,
so they'd all but disappear.
We circled our eyes with heavy black liner
to shut out our fears, and when one of them
approached, we practiced a morgue-like silence.

Girls as pale as cadavers,
while the Vietnam war, insatiable,
escalated like a bloody red maw
waiting to devour the future.
Johnson's lottery setting a boy trap
just outside of the high school doors.

On Catskill Mountain Vacations

How many times did I slip and fall in the brook?
How many brand new outfits muddied,
careening across the flat rocks?
My mother swore and clucked
as she hurried me back to the room
to get cleaned up and presentable,
as the bells were busy ringing
us down to the dining room.

From the overlook near the house
the shadows looked like bathing beauties,
wearing those goofy water shoes
and caps festooned with rubber flowers,
daintily picking their way
along the stony rim of the glen,
wading into the basin beneath the falls.
It was where we swam before the pool was built.

Follow the white arrows into the woods,
and listen to your steps as they thud
drum hollow along the undulant path.

The stream cuts so deep
you have to zig away from its heart,
then zag down the edge of the cleft
on root steps, grabbing at saplings
that stripe the path like stationary walking sticks,
inching you down to where shade hangs cool
in sheets above the numbing gurgle of the brook.

Year after year we listened
for the German man's early morning yodel
as he stepped beneath this icy curtain spilling over the moss.
He laughed and called me little knockwurst once,
as I shuffled to the bathroom out of sleep.

Year after year we hiked there,
making a pilgrimage,
looking for the drinking glass
on its small rock shelf in the cave wall,
holding it close to the place where the spring
runs sweet and clear and steady as the hours.

Under this overhang, you feel nestled in,
as if a giant had scooped you up in cupped hands,
holding this whole place, and you too
up to the sky like a green gift.

But then the shyness sets in.
You feel a bit like a salamander
caught by a quick-handed boy,
with a coffee can and time to kill:
suddenly out of your element,
and apprehensive about what comes next .

But it's good to be out of your element,
washed clean of the city, the job, the world
with all of its burdens and uncertainties.
This place a little bit like Lourdes.

Ghosts return to hover around you here in the mist:
my mother and father taking the freezing wade
hand in hand, gliding along the smooth plateaus,
riding the slippery velour of the under-life
as all their fights and mistakes go floating away
and you see them eternally happy, limned in light.

This is the outpouring of love
that never changes.
How good it is to come back,
touch and smell the earth,
let the water into your bones,
listen to the laughter they left behind.

Paterson By Milk Light

At four o'clock in the morning, one of the copper
statues in front of Paterson's City Hall
got an itch, and climbed down.

It doesn't really matter which one it was.
All of them had been listening to the buses,
shouldering pigeons, or watching bums curl up
on the benches, for so long they all looked alike.
Three stiffs dressed in the verdigris of neglect.

Every step he took produced a terrible
ringing, but he didn't let that stop him.
He labored through the thin milk of a city night,
one foot sliding forward, the other dragging,
east on Market Street, heading toward sunrise,
past Weida's candy store window, full of teddy bears,
looking as inert as he had only minutes ago.

Past the white facade of Bickford's, where sleepy
vacationers ordered bacon and eggs, before
driving off to the mountains, or down the shore.
The smell of coffee seemed so alluring, but he
moved on, crossing Straight Street, plunging
off one curb, staggering up on to another.

The streets were not entirely deserted.
Drunks on their way home, early birds
meandering to work and such, but not once
was there a screech of brakes, or a quiet *I'll be damned*.
Like an old coot staggering home to face the music,
he lurched through the linear world of block after block.

Until he stood at the entrance to Sandy Hill Park,
where light was just beginning to pink the stone walls,
and wind to blow through the wire mesh of the trash cans.

It looked inviting. He found a break in the wall
and followed the path, but it was stepping onto
the grass that changed everything, its curious
texture, its lush beckoning, its greeny welcome,
the way it took his weight on, the cool
shiver, wobble, and bounce of every step.

All those years downtown, with the wacky mayors,
the web of corruption, picketers in sunlight, addicts
nodding under street lamps, hippie kids chanting
no more war, the long race riot summers, He felt
them peeling away, like a rind that had nearly strangled
the fruit. It was quiet. He danced until he fell down,
he laughed and stretched out, feeling light as a leaf.

And that's where two patrolmen, out looking for
flashers, found him, in the shade of two honey locusts.
How did this thing get all the way out here?
They said. *Must be heavy as hell!*

Aunt Aggie Closes Her Eyes

and her soul slips away
like a bolt of dotted Swiss on the breeze
flying higher and higher
toward the Magellanic Cloud.

Good–bye, I say.
Hope you don't mind
that I conjured up such flimsy stuff.
It's just that you were gossamer
compared to our workman's poplin and kitchen oilcloth.

I see her circling the moon
with my father, Aunt Mary, and Uncle Joe.
She offers a wispy hand to my mother
just as she always did. A balm she was,
turning up the day my mother was dying,
and helping her to let go.

Aunt Aggie's soul rises out of sleep,
then whirls like a dizzy mist
toward the grim outline of her parents,
the thin arms of Uncle Allen.

I wave. *Thanks,* I shout, *especially for your knock–knock jokes,*
and for not taking sides when things fell apart.
For serving us your too small Sunday roasts,
so we had to stop for burgers on the way home,
my parents joking and laughing instead of fighting.

You gave me my first Pop Tart.
You taught us all how to face life
with a heart so full of love
there's no room left for the fear.
You kept me in your prayers.
I'll always remember.

She giggles and shakes her head,
then flies off to ride the Milky Way,
glad to be as passé as Christmas tinsel.
So the basket I've lugged around all my life
becomes just a little bit heavier.

A Note to Our Furious Readers

From all of us at Read Furiously, we hope you enjoyed our latest poetry collection, *Silk City Sparrow*.

There are countless narratives in this world and we plan to share as many of them as possible with our Furious Readers.

It is with this in mind that we pledge to donate a portion of these book sales to causes that are special to Read Furiously and the creators involved in *Silk City Sparrow*. These causes are chosen with the intent to better the lives of others who are struggling to tell their own stories.

Reading is more than a passive activity. At Read Furiously, its editors and its creators wish to add an active voice to the world we all share because we believe any growth within the company is aimless if we can't also nurture positive changes in our local and global communities. The causes we support are culturally and socially-conscious to encourage a sense of civic responsibility associated with the act of reading. Each cause has been researched thoroughly, discussed openly, and voted upon carefully by our team of Read Furiously editors.

To find out more about who, what, why, and where Read Furiously lends its support, please visit our website at readfuriously.com/charity

Happy reading and giving, Furious Readers!

Read Often, Read Well, Read Furiously!

A Note to Our Furious Readers

From all of us at Read Furiously, we hope you enjoyed this and every publication of Fury we produce.

There are countless adventures in this world and none of these amazing tales are possible without Furious Readers.

It is with this in mind that we pledge to donate a portion of these book sales to charities that model to Read Furiously through their efforts involved in our community. Those listed are chosen so both intend to better the lives of others who like our philosophy wish to own a story.

Reading is more than a pastime at Read Furiously. Non-profits and the creators we opt to add initiative relies to the world-valued all share because we believe any growth which we compare is instead of our craft, also mature positive change in our local and global communities. The causes we support are valuable to Read Furiously operations because we pride in civic responsibility associated with the act of reading. Each cause has been researched thoroughly through our operatives and read upon carefully by our team of Read Furiously's family.

To find out more about why we do what we do and where Read Furiously lends its support, please visit our website at readfuriously.com/charity

Happy Reading and thank Furious Readers!

Read Often, Read Well.
Read Furiously!